Guess What!

Activity Book 2

with Online Resources

British English

Susan Rivers

Series Editor: Lesley Koustaff

CAMBRIDGE
UNIVERSITY PRESS

University Printing House, Cambridge CB2 8BS, United Kingdom

One Liberty Plaza, 20th Floor, New York, NY 10006, USA

477 Williamstown Road, Port Melbourne, VIC 3207, Australia

314–321, 3rd Floor, Plot 3, Splendor Forum, Jasola District Centre, New Delhi – 110025, India

103 Penang Road, #05-06/07, Visioncrest Commercial, Singapore 238467

Cambridge University Press is part of the University of Cambridge.

It furthers the University's mission by disseminating knowledge in the pursuit of education, learning and research at the highest international levels of excellence.

www.cambridge.org
Information on this title: www.cambridge.org/9781107527911

First published 2016

40 39 38 37 36 35 34 33 32 31

Printed in Malaysia by Vivar Printing

A catalogue record for this publication is available from the British Library

ISBN 978-1-107-52791-1 Activity Book with Online Resources Level 2
ISBN 978-1-107-52790-4 Pupil's Book Level 2
ISBN 978-1-107-52828-4 Teacher's Book with DVD Level 2
ISBN 978-1-107-52795-9 Class Audio CDs Level 2
ISBN 978-1-107-52796-6 Flashcards Level 2
ISBN 978-1-107-52798-0 Presentation Plus DVD-ROM Level 2
ISBN 978-1-107-52799-7 Teacher's Resource and Tests CD-ROM Levels 1–2

Additional resources for this publication at www.cambridge.org/guesswhat

Contents

Hello again!

1 **Order the letters. Look and draw lines.**

1 eLo ___Leo___   **2** dvaiD _____   **3** neB _____

4 iiaOvl _____   **5** aTin _____

2 **Look at Activity 1 and tick ✓.**

		yes	no
1	This is Ben.	☐	✓
2	This is David.	☐	☐
3	This is Leo.	☐	☐
4	This is Olivia.	☐	☐
5	This is Tina.	☐	☐

3 Listen and stick.

4 Look, read and match.

①

②

This is my	nine.
Her	friend.
She's	name's Sue.

This is my	eight.
He's	name's Dan.
His	brother.

My picture dictionary → Go to page 84: Tick the words you know and trace.

Vocabulary and Grammar **5**

5 🔊 **CD1 10** **Listen and circle the name.**

1 Tom / Don

2 Pam / Pat

3 Rick / Nick

4 Katy / Mary

6 🔵(About Me) **Draw and say. Then circle and write.**

This is my friend. His name's Alex. He's nine.

This is _____ .
His / Her name's _____ .
He's / She's _____ .

Look, read and circle the answer.

1

What's this?

(It's a door.) / They're doors.

2

What are these?

It's a pencil. / They're pencils.

3

What's this?

It's a rubber. / They're rubbers.

4

What are these?

They're pens. / It's a pen.

 Think **Look and write**

1

What are ___these___ ?

___They're books___ .

2

What's _____ ?

It's _____ .

3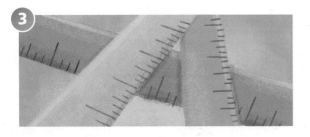

What _____ ?

_____ .

4

What _____ ?

_____ .

Read and number. Then listen and check.

a

Wow! What a big surprise!

And look, Ben! Your lion!

b

This is iPal.

Hello, Ben! Let's play.

c

Stand here. You hold iPal.

d

ROAR!

Oh dear! Help!

Don't worry.

e

This is our treehouse.

We've got a surprise for you!

1

f

Do you like animals?

Yes, I do.

10 What's missing? Look and draw. Then stick.

I play with my friends.

a

b

c

11 Trace the letters.

The rabbit can run.
The lion is lazy.

12 CD1 17 Listen and circle *l* or *r*.

1
l (r)

2
l r

3
l r

4
l r

Value   Pronunciation: *l, r*   **9**

What type of **art** is it?

1 **Look, read and circle the word.**

1

painting /(drawing)

2

photography / painting

3

photography / painting

4

drawing / sculpture

2 **Look and copy the painting.**

Evaluation

1 **Look and write the name.**

L e o | T _ _ _ | B _ _ | O _ _ _ _ _ | D _ _ _ _

2 **What's your favourite part? Use your stickers.**

story   song   video

3 **Puzzle** **What's different? Circle and write.**
Then go to page 93 and write the letters.

_ _ _ _ _
17   10

1 Look, read and tick ✓ or cross ✗.

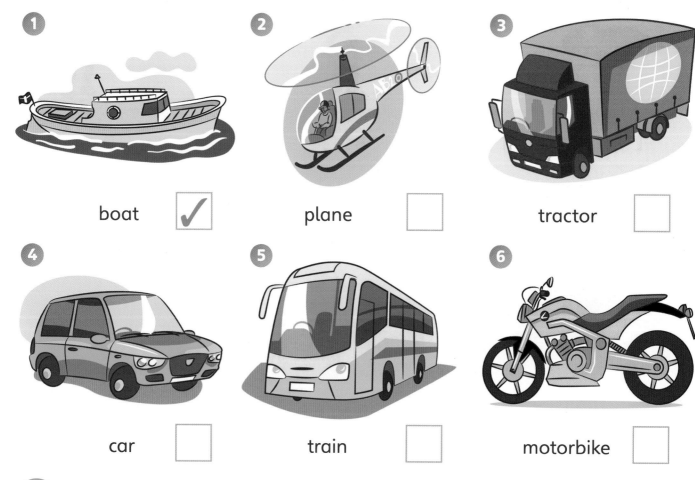

1	2	3
boat ✓	plane ☐	tractor ☐
4	5	6
car ☐	train ☐	motorbike ☐

2 Follow the transport words.

Start →

train	lorry	ruler	chair
desk	bus	plane	camera
book	painting	helicopter	table
pencil	drawing	tractor	boat

Well done!

3 CD1 23 🏷️ **Listen and stick.**

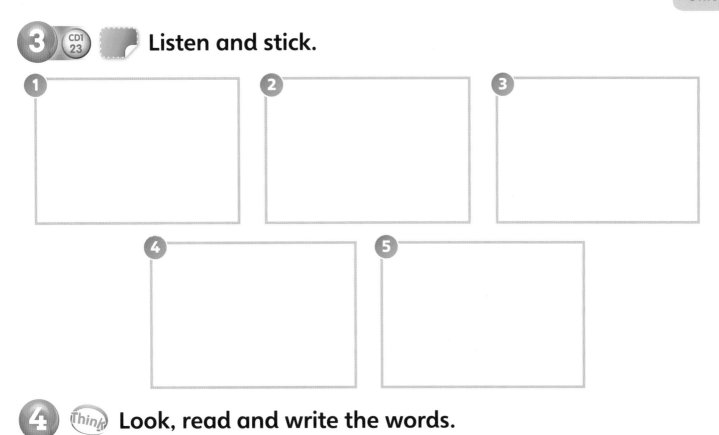

4 (Think) **Look, read and write the words.**

~~lorry~~ boat helicopter car motorbike plane train bus

lorry	

 My picture dictionary ➡️ Go to page 85: Tick the words you know and trace.

5 CD1 26 **Listen and tick** ✓.

6 **Look at the pictures and say.**

In picture A, he's got a car. In picture B, he's got a bus.

7 **Look, read and circle the answer.**

1

Has she got a boat?
(Yes, she has.) / No, she hasn't.

2

Has he got a tractor?
Yes, he has. / No, he hasn't.

3

Has he got a plane?
Yes, he has. / No, he hasn't.

4

Has she got a helicopter?
Yes, she has. / No, she hasn't.

8 **Look at the picture and answer the questions.**

1 Has he got a train?
No, he hasn't.

2 Has she got a boat?
_____

3 Has she got a tractor?
_____

4 Has he got a bus?
_____

9 **Draw and say. Then circle and write.**

This is my friend.
He's/She's got a
_____ .

10 CD1 30 **Read and write the letter. Then listen and check.**

a Yes, of course.   **b** It's OK.   **c** Has Ben got a robot?

d Wow! The helicopter is iPal!   **e** Thank you. This is fun!

f Ben's got a helicopter!

11 **What's missing? Look and draw. Then stick.**

I take turns.

12 **Trace the letters.**

A gorilla in the garden. A hippo in a house.

13 CD1 33 **Listen and match the pictures with *g* or *h*.**

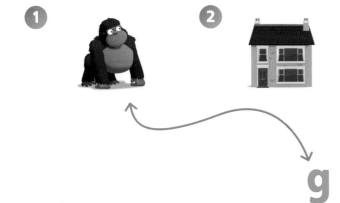

g   **h**

Where is the transport?

1 **Look, read and circle the words.**

1

on land
(on water)
in the air

2

on land
on water
in the air

3

on land
on water
in the air

4

on land
on water
in the air

5

on land
on water
in the air

6

on land
on water
in the air

2 **Look and draw. Say.**

It's a helicopter. It's in the air.

Evaluation

1 (Think) **Look, match and write the word.**

c _plane_

2 **What's your favourite part? Use your stickers.**

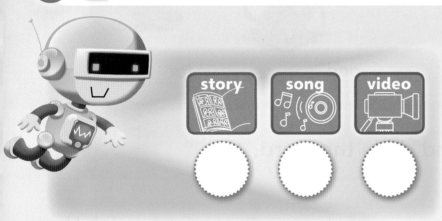

story   song   video

3 (Puzzle) **What's different? Circle and write.
Then go to page 93 and write the letters.**

___ ___ ___ ___ ___
8   1

2 Pets

1 (Think) **Order the letters and match.**

① nma _man_

② lirg _____

③ mwnoa _____

④ yob _____

ⓐ soeum _____

ⓑ hifs _____

ⓒ ogd _____

ⓓ tac _cat_

2 **What's next? Look and circle the word.**

① (girl) / boy

② fish / frog

③ baby / woman

④ cat / dog

3 **Listen and stick.**

4 **Write the words and find.**

1

men

c	h	i	l	d	r	e	n
n	b	j	k	l	o	p	l
b	c	m	e	n	s	a	o
c	y	m	b	c	g	h	j
v	t	m	w	o	m	e	n
m	e	e	t	y	u	k	a
a	w	b	a	b	i	e	s
q	n	e	r	t	f	n	c

2

3

4

My picture dictionary → **Go to page 86: Tick the words you know and trace.**

5 Look, write the words and match.

| ~~ugly~~ | happy | old | beautiful | sad | young |

1 _____ ugly _____

a _____

2 _____

b _____

3 _____

c _____

6 Look, read and tick ✓.

1 2 3 4

1	They're happy.	✓	They're sad.	
2	It's big.		It's small.	
3	She's young.		She's old.	
4	He's beautiful.		He's ugly.	

7 About Me Draw and say. Then write.

This is my cat. It's small. It's beautiful.

This is my _____ . It's _____ . It's _____ .

8 (CD1 43) **Listen and circle the answer.**

Yes, she is. / No, she isn't.

Yes, they are. / No, they aren't.

Yes, it is. / No, it isn't.

Yes, he is. / No, he isn't.

9 **Look at the picture and answer the questions.**

1 Is it beautiful? _No, it isn't._   2 Are they happy? _____

3 Is it ugly? _____   4 Are they old? _____

5 Are they young? _____   6 Are they sad? _____

10 **Look and write the words. Then listen and check.**

cat   ~~frog~~   beautiful   What's   you   sad

1

Look! What's that?

It's a _frog_ !

2

It's Aunt Sue! Hello.

Oh dear! She's _____.

3

Can we help?

Yes, please. I can't find my _____.

MISSING

4

Mr Tom. He's big ... and he's _____!

What's his name?

MISSING

5

_____ that?

6

Thank _____.

You're welcome!

11 **What's missing? Look and draw. Then stick.**

I am helpful. ☺

a

b

c

12 **Trace the letters.**

A fox with a fish.
A vulture with
vegetables.

13 CD1 48 **Listen and tick ✓ v or f.**

1	v ☐	f ✓	2	v ☐	f ☐
3	v ☐	f ☐	4	v ☐	f ☐

What do **animals** need?

1 **Look, read and match.**

1 Animals need food.

2 Animals need water.

3 Animals need shelter.

4 Animals need sleep.

2 **Look at the picture and tick ✓ the box.**

1 A mouse needs shelter.	
2 A mouse needs food.	
3 A mouse needs water.	

Evaluation

1 **Read and write the answer.**

1 This pet can climb trees. It likes mice and fish.	*cat*
2 This pet swims in water. It hasn't got legs.	_____
3 This pet is very small. It has got four short legs and a long tail.	_____
4 This pet likes the water. It's got long legs and can jump.	_____
5 This pet has got four legs and a tail. It isn't a cat.	_____

2 **What's your favourite part? Use your stickers.**

story   song   video

3 **Puzzle** **What's different? Circle and write.**
Then go to page 93 and write the letters.

____ ____ ____ ____
2   14

Review Units 1 and 2

1 **Look and write the word.**

2 **Read and circle the answer.**

1 What are … ?
They're books.
  a this   **b** (these)

3 … babies.
  a It's   **b** They're

5 … she … a boat?
  a Has, got   **b** Got, has

2 He's … a motorbike.
  a got   **b** has

4 How do you … Leo? L-E-O
  a spell   **b** name

6 Is … beautiful? Yes, … is.
  a it, it   **b** they, they

3 Look, read and match.

1

How do you spell Lucy?

2

What are these?

3

Has she got a fish?

4

Are they old?

a No, they aren't.

b L-U-C-Y

c No, she hasn't.

d They're boats.

4 CD1 51 Listen and tick ✓.

1

2

1 Look and match. Then read and colour.

shoes   jacket   dress   T-shirt

skirt   socks   jeans   shirt   trousers

1 Colour the shoes black.
2 Colour the trousers green.
3 Colour the jacket yellow.
4 Colour the T-shirt purple.
5 Colour the jeans blue.
6 Colour the skirt orange.
7 Colour the shirt red.
8 Colour the socks blue.
9 Colour the dress pink.

2 CD1 56 **Listen and stick.**

1 ___

2 ___

3 ___

4 ___

5 ___

3 Think **Look and write the words.**

s̶o̶c̶k̶s̶   jeans   T-shirt   skirt
trousers   shirt   shoes   jacket

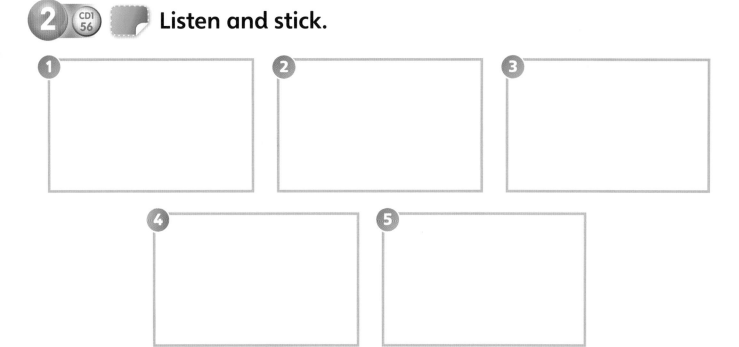

1 _____

2 _____ →

3 _____

4 _____

5 _____ →

6 _____

7 _socks_ →

8 _____

My picture dictionary → Go to page 87: Tick the words you know and trace.

4 Look, read and tick ✓.

1

What are you wearing? I'm wearing trousers and a shirt.

2

What are you wearing? I'm wearing a dress and shoes.

3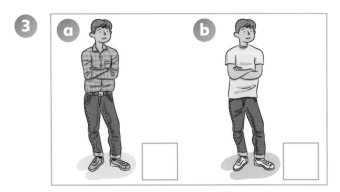

What are you wearing? I'm wearing jeans and a T-shirt.

4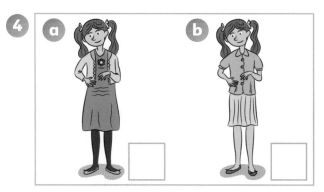

What are you wearing? I'm wearing a skirt and a shirt.

5 Look at the pictures and write.

1
2
3
4

1 I'm wearing ___*a skirt*___ , ___*a T-shirt*___ and ___*shoes*___ .

2 I'm wearing _____ , _____ and _____ .

3 I'm wearing _____ , _____ and _____ .

4 I'm wearing _____ , _____ and _____ .

6 **Listen and number the pictures.**

7 **Look, read and circle the word.**

Are you wearing a (skirt) / **dress**?
No, I'm not.

Are you wearing a **shirt** / **T-shirt**?
Yes, I am.

Are you wearing **shoes** / **socks**?
No, I'm not.

Are you wearing **trousers** / **jeans**?
Yes, I am.

8 **Draw. Ask and answer with a friend.**

Are you wearing a skirt?

No, I'm not.

9 Read and number. Then listen and check.

a. Here you are, iPal. You can use my hat.
Thank you.
And my jacket.

b. Look at these clothes!
Here's a hat for you!
1

c. Look at me!
Fantastic!

d. What are you wearing?
They're clothes for a party!

e. First prize ... The robot!
Thanks. But I'm not a robot!

f. A party?
Yes, look! I'm wearing big trousers and long shoes.

Look, read and stick.

I share things.

 Trace the letters.

 Jackals don't like jelly. Yaks don't like yoghurt.

 Listen and circle _j_ or _y_.

1

j y

2

j y

3

j y

4

j y

What are clothes made of?

1 Look and write the number.

wool ☐   silk ☐   leather ☐   cotton 1

2 Look, read and circle the word.

wool / (silk)   leather / cotton   wool / silk   cotton / leather

Evaluation

1 Write the words and find.

1

socks

2

_____

3

_____

4

_____

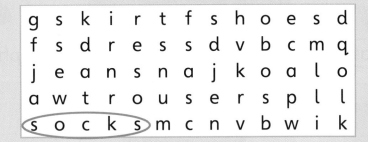
5

_____

```
g  s  k  i  r  t  f  s  h  o  e  s  d
f  s  d  r  e  s  s  d  v  b  c  m  q
j  e  a  n  s  n  a  j  k  o  a  l  o
a  w  t  r  o  u  s  e  r  s  p  l  l
s  o  c  k  s  m  c  n  v  b  w  i  k
```

6

_____

2 What's your favourite part? Use your stickers.

story song video

3 Puzzle What's different? Circle and write.
Then go to page 93 and write the letters.

___ ___ ___ ___ ___ ___ ___ ___
11   12

4 Rooms

1 Look, read and circle the word.

1
wardrobe / (bookcase)

2
lamp / mirror

3
TV / phone

4
sofa / cupboard

5
clock / TV

6
bookcase / table

2 Look, read and write.

1
It isn't a cupboard. It isn't a bookcase. It's a _wardrobe_ .

2
It isn't a mirror. It isn't a lamp. It's a _____ .

3
It isn't a table. It isn't a bed. It's a _____ .

4
It isn't a TV. It isn't a lamp. It's a _____ .

3 CD2 06 Listen and stick.

1

2

3

4

5

4 Think Look, match and write the words.

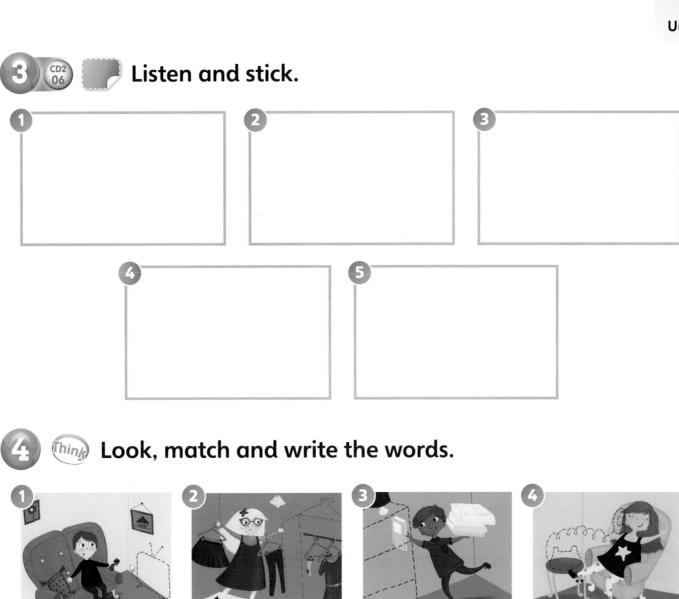

a

b

c

d

_____ _____ _____ _TV_ _____

My picture dictionary → Go to page 88: Tick the words you know and trace.

5 Look, read and write *yes* or *no*.

1 There are four lamps in the bedroom. _no_
2 There are two sofas in the living room. _____
3 There are two clocks in the bedroom. _____
4 There's a wardrobe in the living room. _____
5 There's a bookcase in the living room. _____
6 There's a mirror in the bedroom. _____

6 (About Me) Draw your room and say. Then write.

There's a lamp in my room.

There are two tables in my room.

There's a _____ in my room.
There are _____
_____ in my room.

7 Think **What's next? Read and write.**

fifteen	twenty	~~eleven~~	twelve

1 one, three, five, seven, nine, ___eleven___

2 two, four, six, eight, ten, _____, fourteen

3 three, six, nine, twelve, _____, eighteen

4 five, ten, fifteen, _____

8 **Count and write. Then answer the questions.**

12					

1 How many socks are there?   _There are twelve socks._

2 How many fish are there?   _____

3 How many cars are there?   _____

4 How many shoes are there?   _____

5 How many balls are there?   _____

6 How many books are there?   _____

9 🔵 Read and write the letter. Then listen and check.

a Let's tidy up! **b** Thanks, iPal! **c** It's your ring, Tina!

d Look at this big bookcase! **e** Oh no! Where's my ring?

f Now it's tidy.

1. **e** Is it in the art set?

2. There's my doll. We're in my bedroom!

3. Let's go in. Walk on me!

4. What a mess!

5. Let's put the toys in the cupboard.

6. What has iPal got?

Look, read and stick.

I am tidy.

11 **Trace the letters.**

Meerkats have got mouths. Newts have got noses.

12 CD2 15 **Listen and circle the pictures.**

m

n

How many are there?

 Count and write the number.

1

 +  =

2

 +  =

3

 +  =

4

 +  =

Evaluation

1 **Order the letters and write the word.**

1 mlpa *lamp*

2 abetl _____

3 ccklo _____

4 hepno _____

5 mrrroi _____

6 fsao _____

2 **What's your favourite part? Use your stickers.**

story   song   video

3 **Puzzle What's different? Circle and write.**
Then go to page 93 and write the letters.

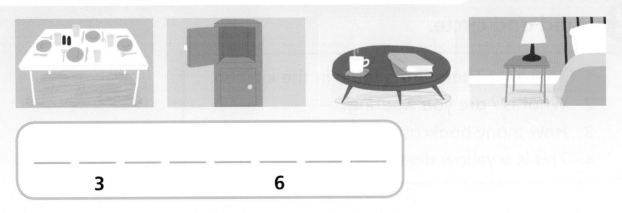

_____ _____ _____ _____ _____ _____
        3   6

Review Units 3 and 4

1 Look and write the word. Then draw Number 9.

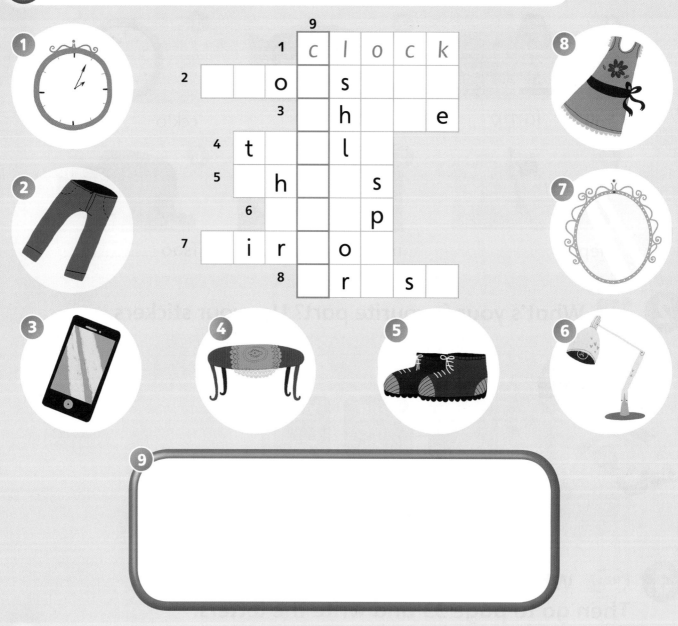

1 c l o c k
2 ___ ___ o ___ s
3 ___ h ___ e
4 t ___ l
5 h ___ s
6 ___ p
7 ___ ___ i r ___ o
8 ___ r ___ s

9

2 Read and circle.

1 **There's** / **There are** a table in the kitchen.

2 What **is** / **are** you wearing?

3 How many bookcases **are** / **is** there?

4 This is a yellow **dress** / **jeans**.

3 Look, read and write the answers.

1

Is it ugly? _No, it isn't._

2

Are you wearing a jacket, Simon?

_____

3

What are you wearing, Grandma?

_____

4

How many socks are there in the wardrobe? _____

4 [CD2 18] Listen and tick ✓.

1

2

5 Meals

1 **Find and circle. Look and write the word.**

1 _____rice_____

2 _____

3 _____

4 _____

5 _____

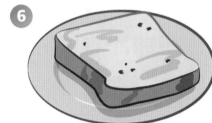

6 _____

peascarrotscereal(rice)toastfish

2 **Look, read and write *yes* or *no*.**

1 There's meat on the table.
   _____yes_____

2 There are peas on the table.
   _____

3 There are potatoes on the table. _____

4 There are sausages on the table. _____

5 There's cereal on the table.
   _____

3 CD2 23 Listen and stick.

1	2	3

4	5

4 (Think) **Look and write the words.**

~~toast~~	cereal	peas	rice	meat
fish	sausages	potatoes	carrots	

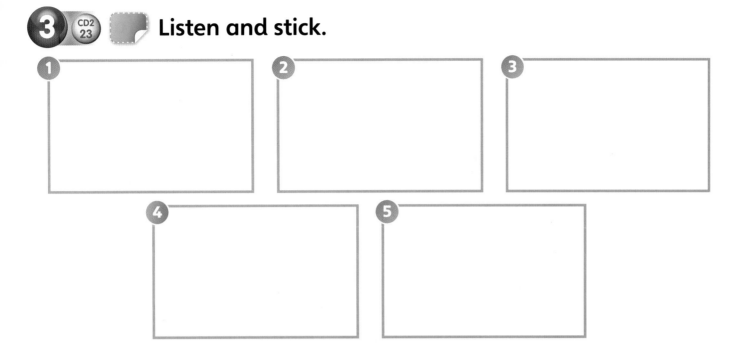

These foods are plants.	These foods aren't plants.
toast	

My picture dictionary Go to page 89: Tick the words you know and trace.

Vocabulary **49**

5 Listen and match. Draw a happy face or a sad face.

6 Look, read and circle the words.

She (likes) / **doesn't like** fish.

He **likes** / **doesn't like** cereal.

She **likes** / **doesn't like** meat.

He **likes** / **doesn't like** peas.

7 **Look, read and circle the words. Answer the questions.**

Kim

Jim

1 Does Kim like (cereal) / sausages?
Yes, she does.

2 Does Kim like **toast** / **peas**?
No, she doesn't.

3 Does Kim like toast for breakfast?
Yes, she does.

4 Does Kim like sausages?
_____

1 Does Jim like **carrots** / **potatoes**?
Yes, he does.

2 Does Jim like **steak** / **fish**?
No, he doesn't.

3 Does Jim like carrots for lunch?
_____

4 Does Jim like potatoes?
_____

8 **Draw and say. Then write and circle.**

My mum likes meat and carrots for dinner. She doesn't like fish.

My _____ likes _____ and _____ for dinner. He / She doesn't like _____ .

9 **Look and write the words. Then listen and check.**

likes   fish   please   ~~lunch~~   peas   Cake

1

Look! Café Hawaii!

Let's go for _lunch_ !

2

Café Hawaii

Would you like _____ and potatoes?

Yes, please!   No, thank you!

3

What about carrots or _____ , iPal?

No, thank you!

4

Oh dear! What would you like, iPal?

_____ ! I like chocolate cake.

5

More cake, _____ !

No, iPal. That's enough!

6

What's the matter?

He _____ chocolate cake – a lot!

52 Story

10 **Look, read and stick.**

I eat healthy food.

11 **Trace the letters.**

A seal in the sun. A zebra in the zoo.

12 CD2 32 **Listen and circle s or z.**

1

S Z

2

S Z

3

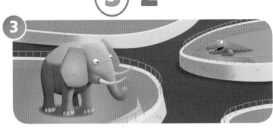

S Z

4

S Z

What type of **food** is it?

1 Look and write the words in the table.

peas sausages rice carrots

fish cheese milk bread

fruit and vegetables	meat and fish	grains and cereals	dairy
peas			

Evaluation

1 **Read and write the word.**

1 T <u>o a s t</u> is bread.

2 C _ _ _ _ _ _ _ are orange. They come from plants.

3 F _ _ _ live in water. They can swim.

4 P _ _ _ are very small and green. They come from plants.

5 Chicken and sausages are m _ _ _ _ .

6 R _ _ _ is small and white. It comes from a plants.

2 **What's your favourite part? Use your stickers.**

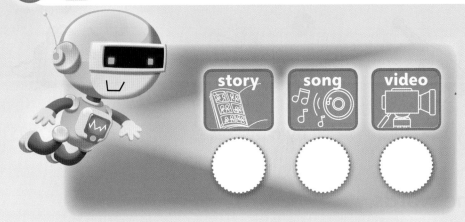

3 **Puzzle** **What's different? Circle and write.**
Then go to page 93 and write the letters.

_ _ _ _ _ _ _ _
4   16

Activities

1 (Think) **Look, match and write.**

 **1**
 **2**
 **3**
 **4**

a ride a _____

b play _____

c fly a _____

d take _photos_

2 **Look and write the words.**

| play | take | ride | fly | play | rollerskate |

 **1**
 **2**
 **3**

A: Let's play tennis. Can you _play_ tennis?
B: No, I can't, but I can _____ basketball.

A: Can you _____ a horse?
B: Yes, I can and I can _____ a kite, too.

A: I can rollerskate. Can you _____?
B: No, I can't, but I can _____ photos!

3   **Listen and stick.**

4   **Look and write the words.**

| ride a horse | ~~play basketball~~ | play tennis |
| rollerskate | take photos | play baseball |

play basketball

 My picture dictionary → **Go to page 90: Tick the words you know and trace.**

Look at the table. Circle the words and write.

	May	Tom	Jill	Sam
✓ **like**	fly a kite	play basketball	play baseball	rollerskate
✗ **don't like**	play tennis	play hockey	ride a horse	take photos

1
I **like** /
~~**don't like**~~
playing tennis.

2
I **like** /
don't like
playing hockey.

3
I **like** /
don't like
riding a horse.

4
I **like** /
don't like
rollerskating.

5 May _____*likes*_____ flying a kite.

6 Tom _____ playing basketball.

7 Jill _____ playing baseball.

8 Sam _____ taking photos.

6 Look, read and circle the answers.

1

Do you like taking photos?

Yes, I do. / No, I don't.

2
Do you like playing tennis?

Yes, I do. / No, I don't.

3

Does he like playing baseball?
Yes, he does. / No, he doesn't.

4

Does she like flying a kite?
Yes, she does. / No, she doesn't.

7 (About Me) Complete the table. Ask and answer.

Do you like horse riding?   Yes, I do.

No, I don't.

Do you like …	riding a horse?	_____ ?	_____ ?
1 Me	yes / no	yes / no	yes / no
2 _____	yes / no	yes / no	yes / no
3 _____	yes / no	yes / no	yes / no

I like …

_____ likes …

8 CD2 44 Read and number. Then listen and check.

a

Well done, Olivia!

Thanks, iPal.

b

I'm sorry.

That's OK.

c

The All Stars are my favourite team!

Let's play! Put on these shirts!

d

Watch me! Throw the ball like this.

Yes!

e

That's not fair!

Play nicely, iPal.

f

It's a basketball!

Are you OK, David?

1

9 **Look, unscramble and stick.**

a   b

I (lypa) _____ nicely.

10 **Trace the letters.**

A camel with a camera. A kangaroo with a kite.

11 CD2 47 **Listen and number the pictures.**

a  ☐

b  ☐

c  ☐

d  ☐

e  1

f  ☐

Value   Pronunciation: c, k   **61**

What equipment do we need?

1 **Look and match the pictures.**

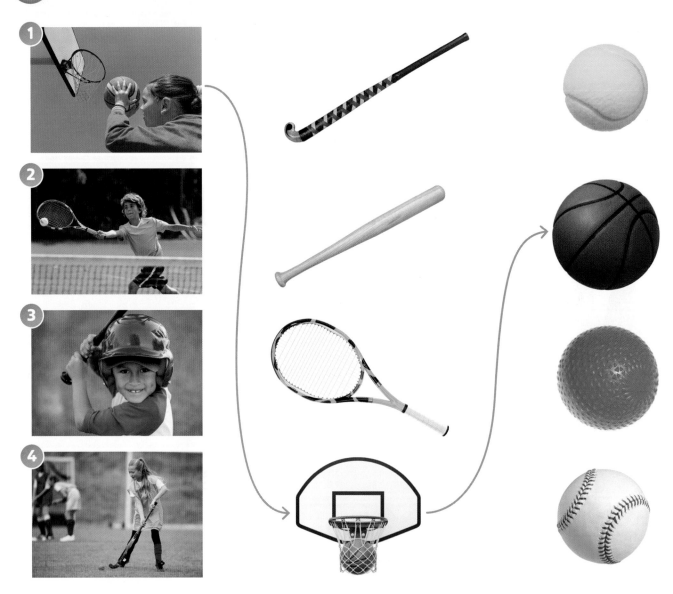

2 **Look at Activity 1 and write the words.**

1 I play basketball with a ___basket___ and a ___ball___ .
2 I play tennis with a _____ and a _____ .
3 I play baseball with a _____ and a _____ .
4 I play hockey with a _____ and a _____ .

Evaluation

1 Think Look and write the activity.

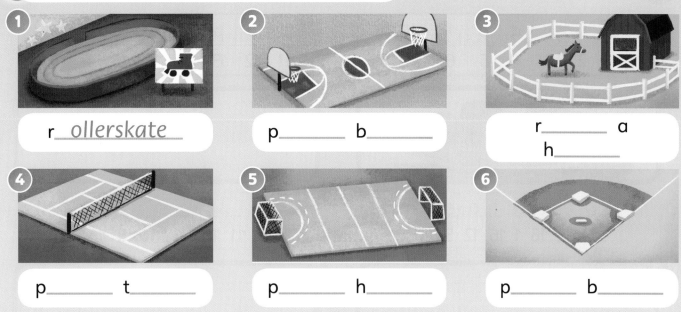

1. r_ollerskate
2. p_____ b_____
3. r_____ a
   h_____
4. p_____ t_____
5. p_____ h_____
6. p_____ b_____

2 What's your favourite part? Use your stickers.

story   song   video

○   ○   ○

3 Puzzle What's different? Circle and write. Then go to page 93 and write the letters.

_ _ _ _ _ _ _ _ _ _ _ _ _ _
15   5

Review Units 5 and 6

1 Write and draw.

a	b	c	d	e	f	g	h	i	k	l	o	p	r	s	t	u	y
1	2	3	4	5	6	7	8	9	10	11	12	13	14	15	16	17	18

1

p o t a t o e s
13 12 16 1 16 12 5 15

2

_ _ _ _ _ _ _ _
6 11 18 1 10 9 16 5

3

_ _ _ _ _ _ _ _
15 1 17 15 1 7 5 15

4

_ _ _ _ _ _ _ _ _ _ _ _ _
13 11 1 18 2 1 15 10 5 16 2 1 11 11

5

_ _ _ _ _ _
3 5 14 5 1 11

6

_ _ _ _ _ _ _ _ _ _ _
14 12 11 11 5 14 15 10 1 16 5

2 Read and match.

1 He likes

2 She doesn't

3 Does he

4 I like playing

5 He doesn't like

6 Do you like

a hockey.

b beans.

c taking photos?

d toast.

e like playing tennis?

f like meat.

3 Look, read and write the words.

rollerskating   rice   ~~photos~~   fish   ~~do~~   doesn't   does   don't

1

Do you like taking __*photos*__ ?

Yes, I __*do*__ .

2

Does she like _____ ?

Yes, she _____ .

3

Does he like _____ ?

No, he _____

4

Do you like _____ ?

No, I _____ .

4 CD2 50 Listen and tick ✓.

1

2

7 In town

1 **Look at the picture and write the letter.**

1 street __e__   **2** café _____

3 school _____   **4** bookshop _____

5 playground _____   **6** supermarket _____

2 **Look at Activity 1 and write yes or no.**

1 There's a toy shop in the town.   __no__

2 There's a playground in the town. _____

3 There's a cinema in the town. _____

4 There's a café in the town. _____

5 There's a clothes shop in the town. _____

6 There's a school in the town. _____

3   **Listen and stick.**

1

2

3

4

5

4   **Look and write.**

1

<u>toy shop</u>

2

3

4

My picture dictionary Go to page 91: Tick the words you know and trace.

5 **Think** **Look, read and match.**

1 next to

2 in front of

3 behind

4 between

 6 **Look, read and circle the words.**

1
The school is **behind** / (**next to**) the playground.

2
The toy shop is **in front of** / **between** the bookshop and the clothes shop.

3
The tree is **next to** / **in front of** the cinema.

4
The supermarket is **behind** / **between** the park.

 7 **About Me** **Draw and say. Then write.**

My school is next to the park.

My school is _____

_____.

8 **Look, read and tick ✓.**

1 Is there a toy shop next to the school?

Yes, there is. ☐ No, there isn't. ✓

2 Is there a café in front of the supermarket?

Yes, there is. ☐ No, there isn't. ☐

3 Is there a toy shop between the book shop and the school?

Yes, there is. ☐ No, there isn't. ☐

4 Is there a playground behind the school?

Yes, there is. ☐ No, there isn't. ☐

9 **Complete the questions and the answers.**

1 _____Is there_____ a park next to the book shop?
No, _____there isn't_____ .

2 _____ a playground between the school and the supermarket?
No, _____ .

3 _____ a street in front of the café?
Yes, _____ .

4 _____ a park behind the supermarket?
Yes, _____ .

CD3 12 **Read and write the letter. Then listen and check.**

a (No, iPal! Be careful!) **b** (I like going to the cinema.)

c (Cinema tickets!) **d** (Oh no! It's closed today!)

e (Look left and right.) **f** (Where's the cinema?)

11 Look, unscramble and stick.

I am (esfa) _____ .

12 Trace the letters.

A quick queen bee. An ox with an x-ray.

13 CD3 15 Listen and write *q* or *x*.

1

*q*ueen bee

2

6

si___

3

o___

4

___ueue

Where are the places?

1 Look, read and circle the word.

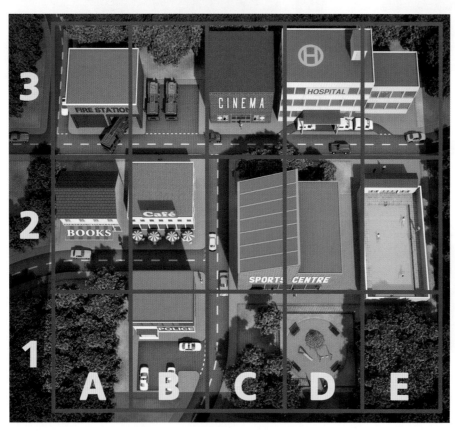

1 There's a (fire station) / **police station** in A3.

2 There's a **cinema** / **bookshop** in C3.

3 There's a **café** / **hospital** in B2.

4 There's a **sports centre** / **park** in D1.

2 Look at Activity 1 and answer the questions.

1 Where's the police station?   _____B1_____

2 Where's the bookshop?   _____

3 Where's the hospital?   _____

4 Where's the sports centre?   _____

Evaluation

1 (Think) **Look and write the word.**

1. _supermarket_
2. _____
3. _____
4. _____
5. _____
6. _____

2 **What's your favourite part? Use your stickers.**

story | song | video

3 (Puzzle) **What's different? Circle and write. Then go to page 93 and write the letters.**

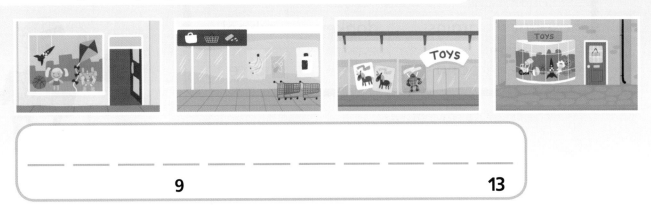

_____

9   13

8 On the farm

1 Look, read and circle the word.

1

cow / horse

2

sheep / goat

3

barn / field

4

horse / donkey

5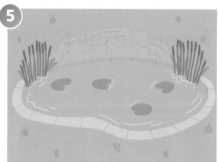

field / pond

6

duck / donkey

2 Follow the animal words.

Start → cow	goat	park	barn
field	duck	sheep	air
hospital	grains	donkey	school
dairy	pond	cat	horse

Well done!

3 CD3 21 Listen and stick.

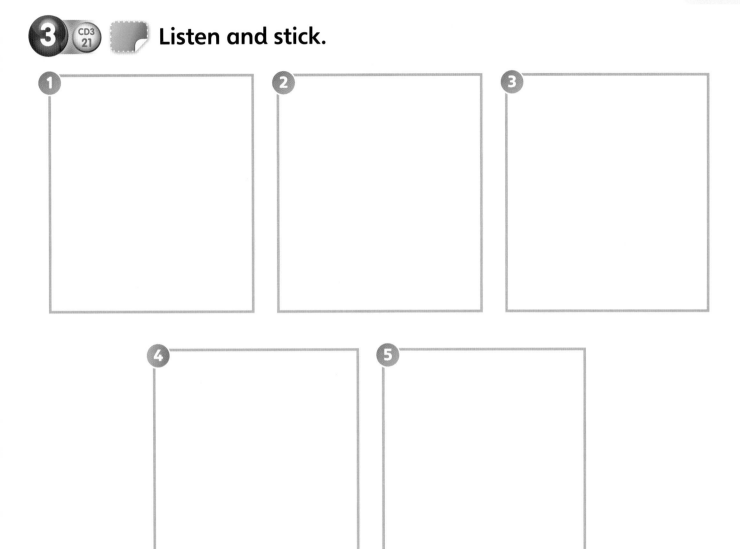

4 Think **Read and write the word.**

1 Milk comes from this animal. It isn't a goat. _____cow_____

2 This animal can swim and fly. It likes water. _____

3 We can ride this animal. It's not a donkey. _____

4 Wool comes from this animal. _____

5 This is a house for cows and horses. _____

6 Fish and ducks swim in this. _____

My picture dictionary Go to page 92: Tick the words you know and trace.

5 Look, read and tick ✓.

1

The cow is eating. ✓

The cow is jumping. ☐

2

The horse is running. ☐

The horse is sleeping. ☐

3

The duck is flying. ☐

The duck is swimming. ☐

6 Look, read and answer the questions.

1

What's the donkey doing?

_____It's eating._____

2

What's the duck doing?

_____

3

What's the goat doing?

_____

4

What's the sheep doing?

_____

7 (About Me) Draw your favourite farm animal. Then write.

This is a _____ .

It's _____ .

8 CD3 25 **Listen and tick ✓ or cross ✗.**

1

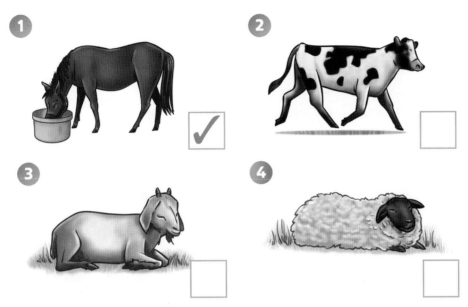

✓

2

3

4

9 **Look, read and circle the word.**

1

Is the horse **eating / sleeping** ?
No, it isn't.

2

Is the cow **running / sleeping?**
No, it isn't.

3

Is the goat **sleeping / eating?**
Yes, it is.

4

Is the duck **swimming / flying?**
Yes, it is.

5

Is the sheep **eating / running?**
No, it isn't.

6

Is the horse **sleeping / swimming?**
Yes, it is.

CD3 27 **Look and write the words. Then listen and check.**

party   iPal   dancing   Goodbye   flying   Welcome

1

It's a message for ___iPal___.

Let's find him!

2

Would you like to come to a _____?

Yes, please!

3

Hold on!

We're _____!

4

_____ to the party!

It's so nice to see you!

WELCOME HOME iPAL

5

What's Ben doing?

He's … _____!

6

_____, iPal!

Goodbye! Thanks for looking after me!

11 **Look, unscramble and stick.**

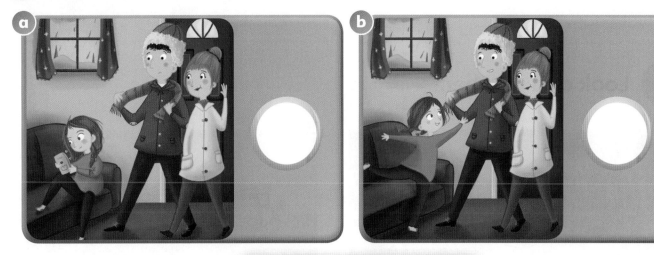

I love my (ehmo) _____ .

12 **Trace the letters.**

A wolf in the water.
A white whale with
a wheel.

13 (CD3 30) **Listen and tick ✓ w or wh.**

1	w ✓ wh ☐	2	w ☐ wh ☐
3	w ☐ wh ☐	4	w ☐ wh ☐

What do **farmers** do?

1 **Look and number.**

2 **Look at Activity 1 and write the letter.**

1 A farmer turns the soil. `b`

2 A farmer plants the seeds.

3 A farmer waters plants.

4 A farmer harvests plants.

Evaluation

1 **Write the words and find.**

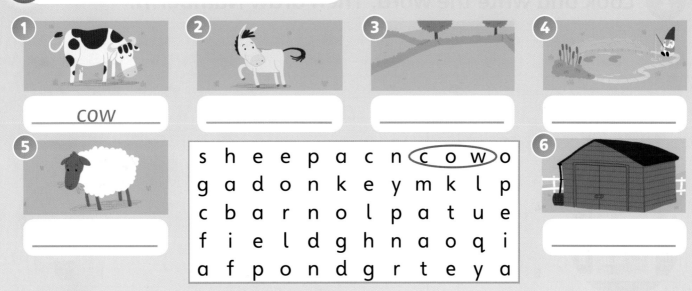

1 _COW_

2 _____

3 _____

4 _____

5 _____

```
s h e e p a c n c o w o
g a d o n k e y m k l p
c b a r n o l p a t u e
f i e l d g h n a o q i
a f p o n d g r t e y a
```

6 _____

2 **What's your favourite part? Use your stickers.**

story   song   video

3 **Puzzle** **What's different? Circle and write. Then go to page 93 and write the letters.**

_____ _____ _____ _____
7   18

Review Units 7 and 8

1 Look and write the word. Then draw Number 11.

1. p o n d

2 Look, read and write the answers.

1

What's the goat doing?

_____It's jumping_____ .

2

Is there a park next to the supermarket?

_____

3

Is the sheep running?

_____

4

What's the horse doing?

_____

3 CD3 33 Listen and tick ✓ .

1

2

83

Hello again!

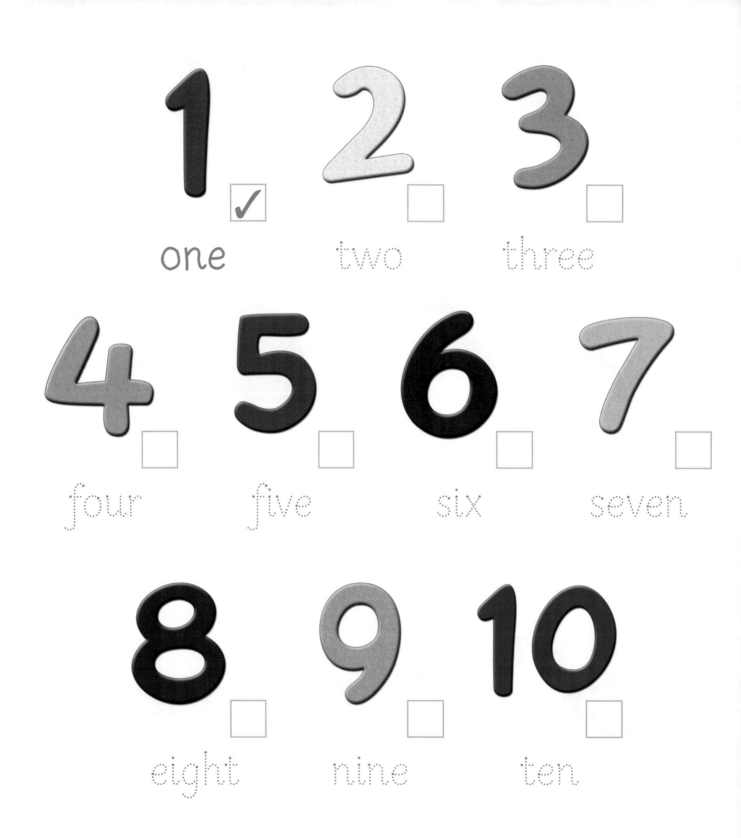

1 ✓
one

2 □
two

3 □
three

4 □
four

5 □
five

6 □
six

7 □
seven

8 □
eight

9 □
nine

10 □
ten

① Transport

bus ✓

boat ☐

car ☐

helicopter ☐

lorry ☐

motorbike ☐

plane ☐

tractor ☐

train ☐

baby

boy

cat

dog

fish

frog

girl

man

mouse

woman

(3) Clothes

 ✓

dress

 ☐

jacket

 ☐

jeans

 ☐

shirt

 ☐

shoes

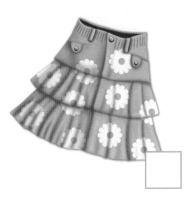 ☐

skirt

 ☐

socks

 ☐

trousers

 ☐

T-shirt

☑

bookcase

☐

clock

☐

cupboard

☐

lamp

☐

mirror

☐

phone

☐

sofa

☐

table

☐

TV

☐

wardrobe

beans ✓

carrots ☐

cereal ☐

fish ☐

meat ☐

peas ☐

potatoes ☐

rice ☐

sausages ☐

toast ☐

fly a kite ✓

play baseball ☐

play basketball ☐

play hockey ☐

play tennis ☐

ride a horse ☐

rollerskate ☐

take photos ☐

(7) In town

book shop

café

school

clothes shop

park

play-ground

cinema

street

supermarket

toy shop

(8) On the farm

 ✓

barn

cow

donkey

duck

field

goat

horse

pond

sheep

My puzzle

1 Write the letters in the correct place.

‒ ‒ ‒ ‒ ‒ ‒ ‒ ‒ ‒ ‒ ‒ ‒ ‒ ‒ ‒ ‒ ‒ ‒ !

1 2 3 4 5 6 7 8 9 10 11 12 13 14 15 16 17 18

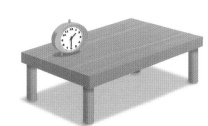

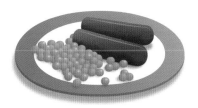